Dr. Tikki A. Collins

Sharing and healing

for Pastors Wives

When The Rib

Is

Broken

Dr. Tikki A. Collins
Table Of Contents

Dr. Tikki A. Collins

When the Rib Is Broken is a registered trademark of Daughters of

Righteousness

Scripture quotations are taken from the Holy Bible, KJV.

ISBN-13: 978-0615945125

ISBN-10: 0615945120

Dr. Tikki A. Collins

Acknowledgements

God gets all the glory. My Lord and savior Jesus Christ has kept me in perfect peace when the weight of ministry and the world became too heavy for me to bare. Thank you Lord for keeping me and being the lifter of my head. Thank you Lord for giving me strength and for loving me when all else seemed empty. Jesus you have been and are truly my savior. To my beloved husband & pastor Calvin Collins, thank you for your guidance, teaching, friendship and your love.......

I thank my family (All of you), especially my mother (Lucia Burrell) for training me up right and always believing in me, my daddy (Earl Burrell) for always allowing me to be his little girl, Mother Dickerson for sharing her heart and her love and all the wonderful Saints of New Bethel Ministries for making my job easy. Aunt Hattie, & Uncle A, thank you for coming the distance, showing your love believing that God can do anything. Aunt Tracey thank you for your story of encouragement as a pastors wife it goes along way. Very special thank you to Gerri Bell and her wonderful husband Elder Eric Bell for being great models of excellence. Much love and thanks to my two besties, Robin Brooks & Cheryle Short, we laugh cry and celebrate together. Thank you to each and every Pastors Wife that shared her story and her heart with me for this project.

When The Rib Is Broken

Pastor's wives and women of God are some of my favorite people in the world! We have a special connection that brings us together in the Lord. As shepherds' wives and servants of God, we have a high calling- a great responsibility. But there is sometimes a taboo that no one wants to talk about as Christian women. I have personally struggled with writing on the subject of the hurts of a married woman of God because for some people the subject is controversial and some feel like the hurts should be swept under the rug.

But, I don't care, there are too many women hurting and hiding behind their faith . There is an error of silence surrounding this issue and someone needs to talk about it. Only in the most intimate of social circles will women of God share feelings and struggles. Then others just grin and bear it hiding behind their pretty clothes and lipstick painted smiles when they really want to cry.

You represent so many of the women who connect with what I write. You represent the women who send me emails thanking me for sharing my heart or asking for advice on whether to file for divorce or fight for their marriage. You represent the women who feel invisible in their marriage. You represent the women who whisper to me at speaking engagements that their marriages are so hard and they don't know if they can stand it even one more day. You represent the women who tell me that they don't know how to love their husbands and be a Christian at the same time because they despise their husbands. You represent the women who remain silent because his cares, wants and feelings are more important than your own. You represent the women who just want to feel the love from your husband that God talks to us about in His word. You represent the rib that is broken. There is a reason that you're broken and it's because the pain is so deep. You have been so very wounded, down into your core. The man that stood before God and vowed to love you more than anyone else, not only did he not love you well, he hurt you over and over again. Sometimes unintentionally, but sometimes he actually meant to do you harm. I have heard the worst stories of hatred living itself out in marriages that I sometimes wonder if these men even know God. And I have witnessed it....so I don't need to ask God to help me imagine. I know the pain. And it's a very unique pain to be a lonely, Christian, married woman.

But know this…you are not alone. There are unfortunately many women who are suffering in silence. There are more women out there than I ever imagined.

When I first started writing this book I began to recall all of the women of God who has shared this hurt with me. Women of God we are unique in our calling. God has equipped us to stand next to these men of God, yet it is a lonely and hurtful walk at times. But we can take joy in the biggest saving grace, we do not walk alone. And when I say that I also mean, Jesus is with us. He has been with us, He is with us now, and He will be with us always.

Chapter One   Bone of My Bone Flesh Of My Flesh

God has given marriage a perfect design and a perfect example

to follow in that Christ represents the groom and the church

represents the bride of Christ. It is the imperfect man that

always fouls up God's design in marriage. God joins man and

woman together perfectly, but something seems to get in the

way. When God created woman He brought her to the man and

the two were married together as one in perfection according to

His will.

Genesis 2:22-24 And the rib, which the LORD God had taken from

man, made he a woman, and brought her unto the man. And Adam

said, This is now bone of my bones, and flesh of my flesh: she shall be

called Woman, because she was taken out of Man. Therefore shall a

man leave his father and his mother, and shall cleave unto his wife:

and they shall be one flesh.

God gave man the perfect plan in the Garden of Eden but even in the garden man somehow found a way to mess up what God made perfect. Yes, we know the story how the serpent deceived Eve and she gave into the temptation of the serpent and ate what God told Adam not to eat. But let's look at that scripture for a minute.

Before God gave Adam a wife He commanded him, "Of every tree of the garden thou mayest freely eat: but of the tree of knowledge of good and evil, thou shalt not eat of it: for in the day that thou eatest thereof thou shalt surely die" (Gen. 2:16-17).

God was talking to Adam in this scripture not Eve. Now, I would like to know why Eve was left alone in the garden feeling vulnerable talking, taking counsel and listening to the voice of someone other than her husband whom had dominion over everything on the earth at that time. Why was Adam not paying attention to his wife? If he was paying attention to her, why did he allow her to take advice from the enemy? Why did he leave her alone allowing the devil to play with her mind?

This is the same question that many pastors wives ask today. Why doesn't my husband pay me any attention, why doesn't he spend time with me, why does he pay more attention to everything and everyone else, why does he put everything else above me the very person that God has given unto him? Why does he cheat? Why does he hurt me and not seem to care? Why am I not good enough? Why can't he see my pain? He is a man of God so how can he treat me so bad? Wow, these are all of the questions that I hear over and over again.

My God fearing sisters we will get through these answers and many more in the next few chapters of this book.

But we must know and understand that God has given us the power to be victorious and the power to overcome even these obstacles. As we find healing for ourselves, and as we understand the power that God has given unto us to become more than conquerors.

The question really is, who do you trust with your broken rib? There are 12 ribs on each side of your chest and they may become bruised, strained, broken, or separated. All of the ribs are attached to the vertebrae (backbone) in the rear. In the front, 10 of them are attached to the sternum (breastbone) by pieces of cartilage. Direct blows to the ribs may bruise or break the ribs or injure the rib cartilage. The ribs may tear away from the cartilage that attaches them to the breastbone. This tearing away from the cartilage is called a costochondral separation.

This is the medical description of what a broken rib is. The definition is in direct similarity to that of a broken married woman's relationship with her husband. Women, we are the rib, the other part of our mate that makes marriage complete. So why is it so lonely in marriage and why is there so much pain as pastors wives?

As the medical description above reveals, when the rib in the physical body becomes bruised or broken it can cause other complications in the body.

Rib injuries usually result from a direct blow to the ribs or chest. Depending on how badly the rib is broken it can most certainly cause separation from the body and tearing away from the body destroying other organs.

This is a great illustration of what a pastors wife feels who is hurt and broken in her marriage. The hurt and the pain becomes so devastating that she begins to tear away from her husband who God says is bone of his bone and flesh of his flesh. When we as women become so bruised and broken that we tear away from our husbands it begins to cause destruction to other areas of our lives.

How can a godly man allow his rib (wife) to be torn away from his flesh? Let us stop right there as that was meant as a rhetorical question. We must understand as women that we have control over what it is we feel as well as what we are willing to allow in our hearts, mind, spirit and in our marriages. One thing for sure is that we cannot control anyone other than ourselves. The question that was asked was how can a godly man allow his bone to be torn away from his flesh?

The answer is not what your husband allows but what will you allow God to do in you. Men can be very complicated at the same time very simple. Women will never understand a man and a man will never understand a woman. I don't care how many books are written on the subject, it is one of the greatest mysteries in the world. But I take comfort in knowing that God knows His sons and His daughters.

I have found that some of the worst marriages are Christian couples. It is mind blowing to see so many Christian marriages failing, especially church leaders. How can so many Christian marriages get to the point of no return if God is at the foundation of the marriage? The answer is simple.....somebody is not allowing God to be the foundation of the marriage. Either the pastor is not submitting to Christ for his marriage, the wife is not submitting to Christ for her marriage or worst, neither one is allowing Christ to be the foundation of the union.

Marriage is a sacred institution unto God Himself. God created marriage, literally! Adam and Eve were created to worship God in the beauty of holiness! God created woman to help man. God decided that man could not do it alone! Yes, God said it, MAN NEEDED HELP!

Genesis 2:18 And the LORD God said, It is not good that the man should be alone; I will make him an help meet for him.

God created the woman to help her husband, not to be mistreated and disregarded as a hindrance or treated as a convenience for sex. NO, GOD SAID MAN NEEDED US!

So why is it that there are so many broken ribs in the body of Christ? Why are so many pastors wives hurting?

First we must realize that God created marriage under the most perfect and holy conditions, in the Garden Of Eden. This is important to understand because this is before the fall of Adam. Marriage was perfect and so was man. After Adam fell, the perfection of marriage and the interaction between husband and wife has changed forever. Adam was the head and worshipped God with the wife that he was given by God. He fell and the perfect marriage went from a place of worship and thriving that was pleasing to God to a place of turmoil, strife and hiding from God.

Genesis 3:8 And they heard the voice of the LORD God walking in the garden in the cool of the day: and Adam and his wife hid themselves from the presence of the LORD God amongst the trees of the garden.

It is separation from God that causes the rib to be broken. We will be unable to heal unless we stay in the presence of God through our hurt, disappointment, resentment, frustration, and our pain. Please don't think that I am saying this is easy to do because I know that it isn't. Maintaining a positive and loving attitude when the enemy is in the garden can be a nightmare but God is keeping sweet dreams alive! We are more than just pastors wives. We are women whom God chose to stand next to the pastor. He chose us to be the help meet. The man of God must understand that we desire more of him to help keep us safe in this fallen garden.

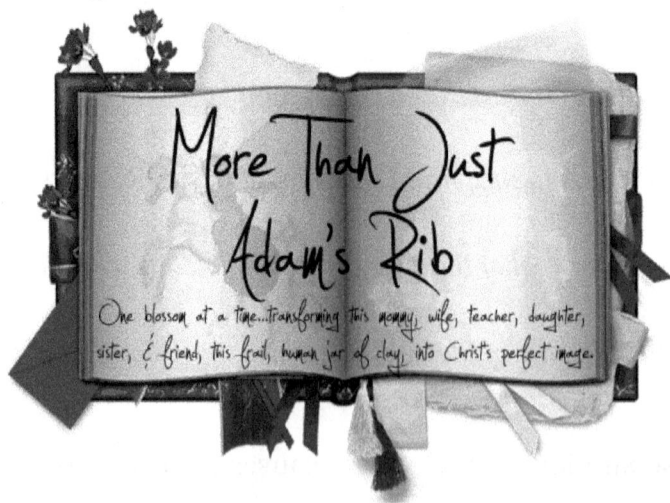

More Than Just Adam's Rib

One blossom at a time...transforming this mommy, wife, teacher, daughter, sister, & friend, this frail, human jar of clay, into Christ's perfect image.

Chapter 2 The Woman Behind The Mask

No one in the church family is more vulnerable than the pastor's wife. She is the key figure in the life of the pastor and plays the biggest role in his success or failure in ministry. And yet, she is treated as an unpaid employee, an uncalled assistant pastor, an always-available office volunteer, a biblical expert and a psychological whiz.

She is almost always a reliable helper as well as an under-appreciated servant.

She is the most vulnerable person in the building. That is to say, she is the single most likely person to become the victim of impossible expectations and pastoral frustrations.

Dr. Tikki A. Collins

The pastor's wife can be hurt in a hundred ways—through attacks on her husband or herself. Her pain is magnified by one great reality: She cannot fight back.

She cannot give a certain member a piece of her mind for criticizing her husband, or members who continue to monopolize his time with the same problems day after day, week after week and some people the same problem year after year. She has to take it in silence, most of the time. Ok, well maybe the silence isn't me but let's keep going.

It takes the best Christian in the church to be a pastor's wife and pull it off. And that's the problem: In most cases, she's pretty much the same kind of Christian as everyone else. When the enemy attacks, she bleeds.

She is the object of a world of expectations …

She is expected to dress attractively, She is expected to be the

perfect role model, to be her husband's biggest supporter and

prayer warrior, and to attend all the church functions faithfully.

Since her husband is subject to being called away from home at

all hours, she is expected to understand this and have worked it

out with the Lord from the time of her marriage—and to have

no problem with it. If she complains about his being called out,

she can expect no sympathy from anyone. If she does voice her

frustrations, what she hears is, "This is what he was called to

do," and "Well, you married a preacher; what did you expect?"

We expect that he would also do what God said for him to do in

his own home! That's what we expect!

The pastors wives I know, down to the last woman, are

concerned for God's glory and for the good of His bride, the church. They would give anything (some of them have given everything) for the kingdom. We don't put on a good face because of a prideful conviction that we must have perfect hair or people will laugh behind our backs. Instead, I believe most of us minimize our own problems because we think revealing them would be harmful to the kingdom. We keep quiet to protect our husbands, to spare the church additional burdens, and sometimes just because nobody even thinks to ask us what's going on.

We share our husbands with hundreds of church members, each of whom feel they own a piece of him. Which is another story altogether. Members don't own your husband and your husband doesn't own the church. It all belongs to Christ.

Dr. Tikki A. Collins

Part of the hurt for pastors wives is that more attention is given to the members than to the wife. Something is seriously wrong with that picture. I said it before, the church is the bride of Christ not the bride of your husband. So much of the discontentment comes because the pastors energy is spent on the church and when he gets home there is not much left for his bride. This is a reason that the rib becomes broken. There is no attention being given to the wife at home. So much life is being sucked out of the pastor or the church leaders with the flock.

I tell my husband all of the time, you are not the Holy Ghost! You can't fix people only God can do that. As a pastors wife, I counsel with other First Ladies and I understand their hearts because we share some of the same burdens that no other woman could truly understand. There was a woman who once told me that she wanted to have a conference for pastors wives, it took me by surprise because not only was she not a pastors wife she despised her pastors wife and she ripped her apart every time she would speak about her! I told her that I would never support her in the conference because she could not even begin to relate to a pastors wife because she did not share our heart. This is a prime example of what I mean. You don't even know the weight that we carry and on top of that you are tearing your own pastors wife apart every chance you get but you want to host a conference! Girl Bye!

We deal with women who are just looking to sleep with our husband, women who want to be where we are, women who cleverly try to get close enough to us just to befriend him and so many other Jezebel filled ways. We are always on guard, and on God, praying and interceding not just for the members and ministry but we have to pray against the demons on a mission to destroy the man of God and the vision

that God has given to our husbands. We have to be their eyes,

their ears and their strength in prayer. We have to carry many

burdens that no other woman could even imagine. It's not that

we complain nor do we even mind for that matter because we

know that God has called us to be the rib at his side in ministry.

But it does not mean that we don't get tired, it doesn't mean that

we don't hurt.

We live in a fish bowl where everyone watches our every move

and waits with baited breath watching to see if we will mess up.

Pastors wives never have a day off.

My husband knows that I am as good as what he helps pour

into me in ministry and where ever it is that my husband falls short with me, I have to ask God to pick up his slack that I may

stay whole in ministry. Because if I'm spiritually depressed, if

I'm crippled by sin, if I'm anxious or angry, I can't do my job.

And when one portion of the body gives up, when the rib is

broken all parts are affected.

A hurting pastor's wife is a hurting church member. She needs

her husband to minister to her, just like any other Christian

woman. And, because her situation is slightly different, because

she is carrying some of the same weight he carries, she needs

more of him. Because he lacks in giving of himself as a husband

at home, she also carries that weight as she walks around hiding

behind a mask pretending that everything is ok in public when

her world is falling apart as he fixes everyone else's.

Dr. Tikki A. Collins

One beautiful pastors wife that I counseled shared her story

with me. She said that the mask was armor for her soul. Her

husband is the leader of a large local church and she is young

and did not expect to find herself on a pedestal, but she did. She

was young and naive and had much to learn. She said "If they

expected perfection and I couldn't deliver, I would fake it". The

mask was part of the job, so she put it on. Like many of us

pastors wives do. I understood her completely because as a

young pastors wife when I married my husband 5 years ago, I

had to learn as I went along. I could hide my whirling doubts ,

questions, weaknesses, immaturity, fear of being misjudged

behind a plastic smile. I just had to say "We're fine, God is

good, appear at all the events, smile, and maintain proper

submissive-wife posture. Then no-one would criticize. But I

fortunately had a husband who helped me navigate through the experience of being a pastors wife. BUT, more than his help, I learned how to depend on God for direction in the areas that I did not know how to navigate. This does not mean that I know or have all of the right answers but I know someone who does, God.

There is a lot of misunderstanding that swirls around pastors and church leaders wives in general, but when coupled with being an introvert, in a church that contains many, many outspoken, judgmental, extroverted saints, the perceptions and expectations can be overwhelming to us.

There are many things behind that mask, that beautiful Sunday morning smile of a church leaders wife that many people could never begin to understand. We love our congregation - just not all at once. We are sometimes judged as unfriendly or snobby and most of the time it is truly not the case. We are very caring, loving women who share the weight of our husbands calling and burdens that no one else but God would ever understand. I am not saying that there are not those type of women serving as pastors wives. I am sure there are many snobs in the kingdom but I believe most of us are loving, nurturing and caring women of God. We are intense feelers and we truly care about those whom God has entrusted to the care of our husbands.

We feel the pain and hurt of each woman in the ministry when she talks about her issues of abuse, neglect, hurt, wayward children, addiction, cheating spouse and the many other issues that she struggles with. We feel the pain of these women because we care but mostly because we too are women and we ourselves have either gone through or share some of the same burdens. We have a few differences. The main difference is that

we stay behind the mask and become everything for everybody,

we help shoulder the weight for everyone else, we get on the

battlefield in prayer too intercede for those who bring us their

trials and we do it with a smile because we are the pastors wife.

We are perceptive and sensitive.

We have our own personal burdens and weights that only God

knows, but we handle everyone else with care all while behind

the mask. Hiding every problem, hurt and disappointment. We

handle it like a pro!

Sunday morning produces a whole lot of handshaking,

hugging, small talk, and interacting with a whole lot of people

all at once, and it sucks out every ounce of her energy. She does

it all with a smile behind the mask depending only on Christ to give her strength at the end of the day. We bear the burdens of

the weak because we are deemed to be strong. God carries our

burdens because no one else will ever understand.

My first lady friend Brandy experienced a different side of

being behind the mask. She said that she was shriveling up like

a snail in salt. She said" I wasn't fine", "God didn't appear to be

good because of all he allowed to happen". But admitting her

struggles wasn't an option.

Brandy said she wanted the mask off... .....I needed it off she

said— it was killing her. But every time that she tried to begin

peeling it off, she felt out of control, she feared that she would

not know what to do without the pretense of the mask. She

learned that if you reveal too much, they'll use it against you. If

you're not perfect, you're not qualified.

This is an extremely heavy burden to carry. No-one told her that the mask is permanent. The worst part is she still tries to live up the high standards of perfection behind the mask. Take off the mask, God already knows who you are, now it's time to show the world the great woman who God equipped for this assignment, flaws and all!

Be encouraged woman of God. There is a reward that you may never see from your husband, or the congregation but God is honoring you through it all.

John 12:26 If any man serve me, let him follow me; and where I am, there shall also my servant be: if any man serve me, him will my Father honor.

Chapter 3 HAVE YOU SEEN ME?

Do you remember that advertisement that came on the back of the milk carton that asked the question have you seen me? The milk carton contained a picture of someone that was missing and the advertisement was put on the carton so that everyone who grabbed that carton of milk would see the face of the person who was missing in hopes that someone would recognize them. I always looked forward to seeing those cartons of milk on my table when I was a teenager. I looked forward to seeing the pictures of the girls on that carton not because it was a good situation but because I always thought that I would be the one to help find them. I use to imagine what she must be going through. The picture on the carton was only a image that someone else posted for the public to see, however the person in the picture had a whole different story than anything my little mind could ever imagine.

Women of God there is a completely different image of who you are and what you are going through that no one knows but you and God. As pastors wives there is sometimes a part of you a very intimate piece of you that is missing. That piece of you cannot be seen by others no matter how much you cry, how much you try to explain, or how much it hurts. There is that image that your husband and the rest of the world will never see or understand.

There is a hurt and a burden that comes with a missing piece. When a pastor or church leader makes his wife feel as if she is not important to him, he creates a missing piece within her. When a husband devalues his wife he creates a missing piece of respect, when he cheats on her he creates the missing piece of trust, when he beats her he creates the missing piece of safety, when he abandons her emotionally and spiritually he creates the missing piece of security. But how can a man of God do so much damage to his wife by creating so many missing pieces? This is such a difficult question to ask but it is a relatively simple question to answer.

I have a very close friend named Alison who have been married for nine or ten years. Alison and her husband look like the most perfect couple in the world. When you see them they are always laughing with one another, attending church together, hosting gatherings at their home and they both love God. If anyone would have told me that they were having marital issues I would have said, "The devil is a lie"! It just goes to show that what you see on the carton doesn't represent what's really going on with the person.

Well, Alison shared with me the hardships that she was going through in her marriage. Of course it took me by surprise because I thought they had it all together. I was wrong!

Nevertheless, she began to tell me how shortly after they were married they started having problems. She said that he had roving eyes, eyes that could not keep off of the backsides of other women. Where ever they went he would always make her feel insecure because he was always looking at other women. She began to feel bad about herself comparing herself to the women that she saw him looking at. Alison quickly began to lose her self esteem what little was left after already half shattered due to other problems that she endured earlier in her life. Now, I am not talking about a weak woman, I am talking about a God fearing woman who overcame some things, and I mean some very, very harsh situations in her life.

One day Alison was in the grocery store with her husband and he was looking inappropriately at a woman who stood in front of him in the line. After her husband paid for his things, Alison and her husband walked out of the store together. The woman who was in line in front of them was walking past them and Alison's husband broke his neck turning around to get one more good look. Well, honey what did he do that for! Alison took off her shoe and hit him in the back of his head, as she should! Of course they began to argue and nothing was really solved because his behavior went on for the next five years or so. Alison was fed up with her husband and she cried out to God more and more because she could not understand what the problem was. She did not understand where she went wrong, she married a God fearing man, a man that loved God, a man who was in his word, going to church, going to bible study, praying, ministering, working hard and loving God. She was married to a God fearing man, so what was the problem with him, she asked God daily!

Alison was tired of the roving eyes and the womanizing ways, she became so frustrated with his ways that she did what most of us would do, she followed him, she broke his windows in his car, she through pots and pans, cried, cut up his clothes, prayed, flattened his tires, prayed some more, locked him out the house, stopped cooking his dinner, stopped speaking to him, cried some more and then repented for her actions and asked God to fix it! This went on for several years of her marriage and she kept crying to God.

About three years ago Alison's husband had to have surgery and they both went to the hospital early that morning to get him checked in and ready for his procedure.

As they completed his procedure he had a bad reaction to the medication that they had given him, it caused his entire body to shake violently. The doctors could not get his body under control from the shaking. They called Alison into the recovery room and told her that her husband was having some serious issues with the medication. Alison began to pray over her husband and the Lord said to her, " Look at him, he is suppose to be the man and he can't even stop himself from shaking, but he is going to be alright". Alison reached over and held her husband and kept praying, he stopped shaking and his body returned to normal. Her husband began to cry and apologize to her for everything that he put her through. I am happy to say that from that moment on he has been a wonderful husband to her and their marriage is totally committed to Christ and one another.

Alison, took her hand off of the situation and allowed God to do what only He knows how to do in a person. Yes, she tried to get her husband's attention by breaking and tearing up things but none of that worked. She kept crying out to God and the moment she quit taking matters into her own hands God delivered her husband into her hands. Meaning that God got her husband's attention and all that he did wrong to her, God allowed her to be his only physical comfort during the worst time in his life. When the doctors didn't know what to do, God knew exactly what to do.

It's hard to go through the misery of a cheating man and the hurt that comes along with it but when you decide to stay, God is expecting you to do the things that He requires of you regardless of what the husband does. If you are crying out to God, trust that He will hear your prayer.

Dr. Tikki A. Collins

It does not matter how hard it gets, you must trust God for your marriage if God has told you to stay. Remember God told Hosea to marry a whore!

The beginning of the word of the LORD by Hosea. And the LORD said to Hosea, Go, take unto thee a wife of whoredoms and children of whoredoms: for the land hath committed great whoredom, departing from the LORD. Hosea 1:2

Can you imagine God telling you to go marry a thief, a pimp, a murder, or a crack addict? How do you think Hosea felt after hearing the command of the Lord? He must have been so shocked, yet Hosea obeyed because God was using Hosea's life to teach Israel a lesson.

No matter how much God blessed Israel, they kept turning away from Him.

41

They kept rejecting God for their own sinful lust and pleasures. In the Book of Hosea, Gomer would run off with her lovers (like Israel and us), but God would always send Hosea to get her.

"Go, show your love to your wife again, though she is loved by another man and is an adulteress. Love her as the LORD loves the Israelites, though they turn to other gods and love the sacred raisin cakes" (Hosea 3:1).

Then Hosea would bring her home and ask her to promise she will stay.

"2 So I bought her for fifteen shekels of silver and about a homer and a lethek of barley. 3 Then I told her, "You are to live with me many days; you must not be a prostitute or be intimate with any man, and I will behave the same way toward you" (Hosea 3:2-3).

Later on, Gomer would disappear again, like Israel and (your husband). Even though Israel suffered when they sinned, they refused to repent. But God tells Israel to return and if God has told you to stay in your marriage, He will do a work in your husband just as He did in Israel. He will get his attention in His time, and in His way, you can't force it. Just as Hosea could not make Gomer behave, you cannot make your husband behave. BUT, trust and believe me, better yet trust and believe God, He will get your wayward husband back to his rightful place as a husband. The key is allowing God to do the work, not you.

Hosea "1Return, Israel, to the LORD your God. Your sins have been your downfall 4 "I will heal their waywardness and love them freely, for my anger has turned away from them."

What God wants us to understand from His illustration with Hosea and Gomer is that He can bring about faithfulness, change in our marriages when we get out of the way and allow Him to be God. God sees what your husband is doing to you, He also sees how you are handling the situation. God knows that you are not trusting Him with your husband when you decide to take matters in your own hands. You are going to pay the price if you don't hold up your end of the bargain with God. God gives you the word just as He gives your husband. We have to listen and move the way God says to move or we will not reap the harvest that God is sowing on our behalf.

Women of God we can get so very distracted by the weight of the world that surrounds us. However, we can minimize the distractions by praying, reading the Bible, talking to other Christian women, and following our purpose.

The only way to get victory is to let God have His way,

sometimes it will get hard but your victory depends on it!

Chapter 4   SURVIVING JEZEBEL

The spirit of Jezebel is alive and operating in every church. If

you have not had one in your church yet, get ready because she

will eventually show up. These women come to destroy the

man of God and his marriage. The enemy has an assignment.

It's amazing to me that these women walk so boldly into the

church under the pretense of holiness. She swerves and twerks

her way into the sanctuary with the pastor and other church

leaders in her site. Yes, you know her. She is the one that has a

different problem every week to get the pastors attention. She is

the one that leaps over the pew seats to be the first one to

congratulate the pastor on the word that has been preached. She

is the one that acts as if there is no one else in the universe that

can help her with her issue but the pastor . Yes, you know her, she is the Jezebel that has decided to have an affair with the pastor or the minister.

Unfortunately, this happens too much in the church today. I hear so many stories from women who are battling these Jezebels who come to steal and destroy marriages. The problem is that we as women of God don't use the authority that God has given us to rebuke those demons. We act as if we have to stand by and watch as our husbands are seduced by these Jezebels.

Most pastors wives or ministers wives are afraid to draw attention to these spirits because they don't want to cause problems. They quietly talk to their husbands about their concerns or they just bury their heads in the sand to not ruffle feathers within the ministry. The problem is most men act as if they don't see this Jezebel spirit, they are oblivious and are convinced that the woman is just being polite.

We as women know the advances of a woman. Men are attracted to the flattery of the Jezebel and will not want to recognize it as anything harmful. She knows how to gently stroke his ego. She plays the victim to gain his attention and plays on his desire to be a hero. There is a super hero complex that most pastors and church leaders have to save a damsel in distress. Well, Jezebel is no damsel but she will put him in stress and dam him to hell if you allow her to operate.

I personally experienced a Jezebel who walked through the doors of our ministry. I remember one Sunday morning sitting in the pulpit listening to my husband preach a dynamic word from God and in walked Jezebel!

As soon as I saw her, the Holy Spirit said to me "Jezebel". I politely went over to greet her after service and welcomed her to the ministry. She was dressed in an extremely form fitting, freak- um dress with her assets clearly being displayed. No judgment passed because after all she did come to praise the Lord or did she? No, she had her sights set on a different agenda.

She continued to come back each Sunday and we continued to love her as any other child of God. One Friday night we had a women's fellowship at the church and the men had a fellowship also. We were in one part of the building and the men were in another. As we sat around the table dissecting the word of God and sharing our stories of struggles as women, Jezebel made her first move.

She was constantly reminding me that women could do nothing for her and that her only interest was in the men of the ministry. She said that fornication was not a sin and that we take the bible out of context with sex. Of course her comment caused a big uproar amongst the women.

The sisters began to take her to the word of God and began to explain what God expects. The more they explained, the more agitated she became until she finally said, "Listen you women can't tell me anything, only a man can tell me about the word of God". Did she say what I thought she said? Well as God would have it, my husband just happened to be walking through the room where we were gathered. All of the women began to yell "Pastor"! I politely stopped my husband and said would you please explain to our sister that fornication is a sin because she will not allow us to minister the word through the bible because

50

we are women. My husband began to speak to her in his very

nice calm voice, taking much too long to deliver our message to

this woman. Myself as well as the other women were in an

uproar because of this woman's behavior and we wanted the

pastor to give it to her straight. We did not want him taking his

time, examining his words as not to hurt her feelings. I then

confronted my husband and said "Pastor just tell her it's a sin"!!

The other women began saying "Yes Pastor tell her it's a sin" It's

not that my husband wasn't going to tell her, but it was the way

he was choosing his words carefully and his tone was too

pleasing with her. The women saw the urgency to rebuke her in

love but pastor was being too polite and finessing his words.

Finally one of the sisters yelled out "Pastor just tell her it's a sin"!

Finally pastor recognized our frustration and said "Yes it is a

sin" and before he could chase his words with more of his

niceties, we told him that was all we needed and he could leave the room. See, what we saw as women was the Jezebel spirit but he did not. He just saw a soul that was a woman, but we saw Jezebel. She continued to come to ministry and I continued to pray that God remove her from the bondage that she was under. She continued to bring that Jezebel spirit every time she came. That spirit ended up taking captive several of the men in the ministry. She was able to bed a few of them. The women continued to pray for her and we called her on her behavior. Of course she refused to listen because we are women and she had no use for us. She continued to be disruptive in the ministry. She insisted that she would only take counsel from the men. She would sit in the center of the church with her legs wide open, no panties and a dress on.

I went as far as to give her a blanket to cover herself. I began to understand through the wisdom of the Lord that this spirit could not be pacified, it had to be rebuked.

God allowed me to speak to her spirit and let her know that I saw her and I knew what she was up to. I called out Jezebel and told her who her victims had been. I prayed for the woman who was in bondage to the spirit. She left the ministry. I called her a few times to check on her spiritually, she is still just floating around looking for her next victim.

Women of God, don't be afraid to call out behavior that looks suspicious. Be mindful to seek God and don't be ruled by your feelings. However by all means rebuke the behavior especially when she displays it towards your husband.

Too many women sit back and watch as their husbands cozy up with the church secretary or the sister who has all the problems or whomever Jezebel may be operating through at the time. You have to stand guard, watch and pray as the bible says.

Luke 21:36 Watch ye therefore, and pray always, that ye may be accounted worthy to escape all these things that shall come to pass, and to stand before the Son of man.

If your husband is spending too much time with any sister in the ministry, start asking questions and discern through the wisdom of God if it's appropriate behavior. Pastors and leaders who encourage and want these illicit affairs will make every excuse to cover up what they are doing. Do not be deceived, do not stand by and watch as Jezebel wreaks havoc on your husband and your family.

A man of God or minister who has nothing to hide will welcome your conversation about any behavior that you may view as inappropriate. As his wife he will respect your opinion even if he does not see it for himself he will begin to watch.

So many pastors wives just sit back and allow too many other women access to their husbands simply because they are the pastor. This is not the will of God. God said in His word that the man must make his home his priority, his wife.

We are our husbands eyes in areas that he can't see. He is our covering in life and we are one. Together we are powerful in Christ but divided we are broken. The bible says don't let anyone separate you.

Mark 10:9 What therefore God hath joined together, let not man put asunder.

Don't allow Jezebel to tear up your marriage. Confront that spirit in the name of Jesus Christ. Let it be known that you know what she is up to. If anyone is going to be uncomfortable it's going to be her through the blood of Jesus.

Fight her in the spirit she will not win. Never be afraid to let it be known that you are the wife because you are. No other woman has the right to consume that much attention and time of your husband. If he likes the attention or if he encourages it, he is under the influence of the Jezebel spirit and you must pray for him as well and have the other men in the church who are strong in Christ praying for your husband. Let's stop sweeping these things under the carpet. This is why we have so much adultery in the house of God and it's shameful. God is not in that mess and it must be exposed. I don't understand why there is so many leaders in the church committing adultery.

These people are hearing from God and laboring for God but yet they have time to hear from the devil of lust. There is something wrong with this picture. You are a part of a team when you are married and the devil wants to tear apart the union. He is sending the spirit called Jezebel on a mission to destroy God's men. The devil has a woman for every man of God, it's just a matter of time before she shows up at your church. Let us continue to watch and pray for our husbands and have the courage to walk in the authority to call out and rebuke that Jezebel spirit. *Revelation 2:20-21 But I have this against you: You let that woman Jezebel do what she wants. She says that she is a prophet, but she is leading my people away with her teaching. Jezebel leads my people to commit sexual sins and to eat food that is offered to idols.*

Chapter 5   **Will The Real Leading Lady Please Stand Up**

There is a song called Super Woman by a singer named Karyn White. It is one of my favorite songs. I can relate to this song on so many levels. One of the verses in the song says, "I'm not your superwoman, I'm not the kind of girl that you can let down and think that everything is okay. Boy I am only human. This girl needs more than occasional hugs as a token of love from you to me". I know that so many pastors wives can relate to this song.

There are so many times that as pastors wives we do so much to help the ministry that God has called our husbands to. We work tirelessly because we love God, we love our husbands and we love the people of God. We labor the way we do because we believe in the vision that God has given to our husbands.

We teach, Sunday school, Children's church, Women's ministry, Music ministry, this ministry, that ministry and we do it all with a smile and the love of Christ! Too many times than not we get disappointed. Yes, I know everyone gets disappointed from time to time, however when a pastors wife becomes disappointed it hits home on so many different levels. We can handle the disappointment, the back biting, the criticizing of our husbands and the looks of disgust from the members, because it's all a part of our assignment. The thing that we have a hard time handling is the lack of attention and the disappointment that comes from the man that we love. The giving of ourselves is truly unto God. There is nothing that we expect in return from the people of God, but there is something that we expect from the man of God. More times than not that expectation goes un- met. It is at minimum an expectation of wanting that same love and attention that is given to the flock. That same time and passion that is poured into the church members to be also poured in to us, to help us as we help bear the burdens that we help our husbands carry.

Some pastors and church leaders are able to wear both hats. The husband hat and the pastor hat. Some try their best to wear them both but are only successful at really wearing the one. The pastors wife wears a multitude of hats and she wears them well. I am not saying that we wear them all well all the time, I am simply stating that we are almost always willing to be available and present for the people of God just as we are for our husbands when they needs us. No one truly understands the heart, struggle and cares of a pastors wife, except a pastors wife.

Our work in the vineyard is sometimes envied and sneered upon because other women want to do what we do, but do they really? There are those who sit back and criticize us but when it's their turn to step up to the plate to help, they won't or they can't. We deal with those who sit back and critique our performance yet they don't have the courage to do any of it!

There are those who think that somehow what we do is glamorous. How wrong they are. What they don't understand is that when no one else steps up to the plate to help our husbands carry out the vision that God has given them, we will. Even if it means that we have to do everything. We will see to it with the strength of God that it gets done.

We allow God to direct us that we can close as many gaps as possible in ministry. God uses us, the help meet the needs of the flock and the ministry. We don't expect nor do we ask for recognition. I work because I am a servant, I serve because I love God and I believe in the vision that was given to my husband. As pastors wives there are many whispers that we hear that we have to shake off. There are those women who just come to tear us down and to under mind the ministry. We must understand that everyone in the ministry will not like us. The hearts of some people are treacherous. The hardest thing to do is deal with envious, bitter women. You can't get rid of them so stop trying. They only come to make you stronger. God has given me a tougher skin. I am fairly fortunate because most of the women that God has surrounded me with are wonderful. There have been a few to test me but to God be the glory. He has equipped me to handle them through prayer and love.

There was one woman in our ministry and I won't mention her name, she thought that she was the pastors wife.

62

My husband was in ministry before we were married and she was an Elder in the ministry. After my husband and I were married I looked to her for leadership and guidance. I was very new to serving in the church and excited about doing the work of the Lord. There would be times that I would go to her and suggest an idea for the church or a program within the ministry, and she would never seem interested. She never offered any input or guidance. After several months had gone by and many days of prayer and asking God for direction in this new role of pastors wife, the Lord spoke to me and told me to move forward with a ministry for the women. There had never been a women's ministry within the ministry before and this was going to be the first. I spoke with my husband and he thought it to be a great idea. I expressed the idea to the Elder to get her on board so that we could work together in this new ministry.

She told me that she would be the head of any women's ministry. I was taken back with her attitude and the fact that she had never before wanted to work with the women and now all of a sudden she wanted to be in charge of the women's ministry. Now, keep in mind I was newly married and wanting to work and help the ministry in any way that I could. So I decided to take the back seat and allow her to run the women's ministry. Four months went by and no women's ministry, no activities, no plans, no meetings, no NOTHING! I went to her and asked if there was anything that I could do to help get it going and she said no. After a few more months went by and no women's ministry manifested, I prayed and went back to my husband and expressed that I wanted to take the lead on the women's ministry. My husband agreed and empowered me to start the ministry.

The ministry was birthed and the conflict with the Elder began. It is not my intention to drag her down, however, I want this book to be a real indication of what we go through and share common experiences as pastors wives.

The conflict with this woman began. She really thought that she was the pastors wife. She would say that he was not giving her enough attention and it was really just a weird situation. She was the main woman as far as a leader in the ministry before I came into the picture. She refused to let go and allow me to work. All I wanted was to work with her, not against her. She did not want to work with me. She wanted to be the pastors wife. She wanted to be beside the man of God. It was totally awkward, it caused tension and division in the ministry. So much division that she began to start her own women's ministry in her home to compete with the ministry in our church.

She tried to recruit many of the women in our ministry, she caused a couple of the sisters to leave the church because of her drama. All because she wanted to assume the role of the pastors wife. I am not saying that she wanted to be married to him, I am saying that she wanted to have the role that went along with being married to the pastor as well as the pastors attention.

 If we think for one moment that the enemy is going to allow us to serve in peace, we are already deceived.

Don't think for a minute that every eye that watches us so closely are eyes of love and adoration. Many of those eyes are staring and waiting for us to make a mistake falling from the pedestal that they put us on. I remind myself that I am here to serve God and His people. I am here to be a help meet to my husband.

This is the place where we need our husbands to understand our needs. In the process of us helping our husbands, we get weighed down. God says that we can cast our burdens onto his shoulders, and I get joy from that. God also tells us to submit to our husbands. In our submission God is expecting us to be cared for. The position of the husband in the home and his related responsibilities are quite clearly defined in principle in *Ephesians 5:22, 28-31. "Wives submit yourselves unto your own husbands, as unto the Lord. For the husband is head of the wife, even as Christ is head of the church; and he is the savior of the body. Therefore as the church is subject to Christ, so let wives be to their own husbands in everything. Husbands, love your wife as Christ also loved the church and gave himself for it . . .* So husbands should care for us and love us as their own bodies.

The problem is that many of the pastors are loving the body of Christ but not their wives. God tells us to submit because He has given our husbands the ability to care for our needs. When we need to be poured into, he has equipped him to do so, when we need that extra time, he has equipped him to provide it to us, when we just want to be held because we are needy in that moment, God has given him the strength to provide us comfort.

So many men go around saying, "A wife is suppose to submit", yes we are, and we want to. We also want to trust that you are going to do what God has told you to do with us in your care.

We are not the kind of girls that you can let down and think that everything is ok, boy we are only human. This girl needs more than an occasional hug and kiss from you. We need our husbands to minister to us, pray with us, make time for us and love us in a way that we understand that he feels our heart and

to know that we are truly counting on him.

Chapter 6 The Adulterous Church Leader

This is God's divine plan, plain and simple. Mix these up and you've got major problems. Before God ever created the church, He created the family. Before God ever created the family, He created the marriage. Before God created anything, He was! Man tries to reverse this divine order. It is so critical for you to understand God's divine order. So many pastors have destroyed their own marriages and families because they didn't understand God's divine order.

What does all this mean? I'll get right to the heart-of-the-matter... many people make the mistake of placing the church before their family. I love the church. I am not trying to diminish the church. I am simply saying that the church should never come before your family.

Dr. Tikki A. Collins

I am simply saying that the family should never come before your marriage. I am simply saying that your marriage should never come before God. Many husbands and wives place their family before their marriage. This is not good. Many marriages have been destroyed by a meddling mother-in-law. You are married to one another not your mother.

Many marriages have been destroyed by the church. The pastor does not know how to draw the line between his family and the ministry.

The devil has deceived the pastor who thinks that because he is preaching the gospel and taking care of the people of God that he will be excused for letting his marriage suffer. That was not God's plan. The Bible seeks to strengthen marriages, families and churches... the Devil works to destroy them.

71

Men of a God sometimes let their guard down and forget this fact. There is a dangerous tendency in churches for people especially women to idolize the pastor above their own husband. This is not good! Equally pastors ignore their own homes because he feels as if the church is his wife. It is wrong and sinful for a pastor whether it be a woman or a man idolize or put the church before their marriage.

This is God's divine order, God, home, church! It's as simple as that! Nothing but nothing should ever come between husband and wife... nothing! No person or group should ever separate a husband and wife. Notice that nowhere in the Bible does it say that God has joined us to our family, our neighbors or our church. God has only joined the husband and wife, thus it is to be the strongest of all relationships. Unfortunately, society has launched an all-out attack on the marriage.

It is unfair for a wife to suffer because her husband spends more time at the church then he does pouring into her and his family.

So again, no one should ever come between a husband and wife! This is what God says!

Therefore shall a man leave his father and his mother, and shall cleave unto his wife: and they shall be one flesh. Genesis 2:24

The problem is that some pastors and church leaders don't understand what cleaving means as it pertains to marriage. They cleave to everything else except for their wives. This means that no one should be able to divide your marriage! This means that the church does not occupy the space that is reserved for marriage. The pastor is adulterous when he spends more of his time with the bride of Christ then he does his own bride.

The church is a "called out assembly" of believers, a place where Christians meet, a headquarters for soul winning. Pastors are expected to attend to the needs of the flock when they arise, BUT not when the same need is not being met in his home. How can he take care of the needs of the church when his wife and family are suffering at home? This is truly against the will of God.

1 Timothy 3:5 For if a man know not how to rule his own house, how shall he take care of the church of God?

God ask this question in 1 Timothy for a reason. There are many pastors who try to manage the church like superman and they treat their homes like Kryptonite.

Their wives are broken, their marriages are a mess! God knows what's best and if He wanted the pastor to spend more time with His church than with his own wife, He sure would have written it in His word! I do not understand how a man of God can pour so much into other people and leave so little for the wife in which God gave him. Something is wrong with that picture. Though the pastor often times will never own up to leaving his wife void, God is taking notice. Anything that occupy's the time of another, stealing time from something that should rightfully have that time is adulterous.

Women who are married to pastors are often broken. I hear so many times from the pastors wives the struggle of feeling abandoned. This is a real problem. God does not need the pastor to be the everything for His bride, Jesus is capable of that. God only ordained the pastor to feed the sheep, not take it as his own.

Marriages are under fire and attack and the devil is getting craftier at his devices. Pastors think that because it's church business that it's justified to abandon his home. The devil has deceived him in his thinking. He has him fooled into thinking that he is doing God's will just because it's church. This is a very subtle deception that pastors fall for because it's under the disguise that he is doing God's work. Remember this is the same Satan that tempted Jesus. The problem is that Jesus knew his assignment and He knew his responsibilities of what God required of him. Unfortunately pastors do not know, nor do they see the enemy in this trap. It's sad but it's true.

The pastor thinks that there are choices to be made between the wife and the work of the church. She is a part of that work. The church often times becomes a mistress to the pastor.

The pastor has to realize that a good family home relationship will not happen by mistake. A happy home is no accident, it happens because of the work he puts in at home! It is a shame when the wife or family has to schedule time with her husband but the church and everything else flows daily.

We are living in the last days and Satan is going after the strongest unit on earth which happens to be the family. Separation of husband and wife at the hands of the enemy using the church as his vice.

Pastors WAKE UP! Look at the word of God and ask God about His divine order. He will reveal it. A true man of God will seek God for His family, not just in prayer but in action of God's word.

It is my prayer that pastors and church leaders will pick up this book. It is my prayer that they will turn back to their wives. It is my prayer that God sets in order the marriages that He ordained.

She
IS CLOTHED IN
strength
AND
dignity,
AND SHE
laughs
WITHOUT FEAR
OF THE FUTURE.

PROVERBS 31:25

Chapter 7 YOUR LOOKING AT THE WRONG MAN

Missing pieces are often times already planted from prior relationships and experiences that we have been through, we are just good at burying them. Just like my friend Alison, she endured an abusive cheating relationship with another man before she was married. Those hurts and scars were buried until her new husband started looking at other women and now those old wounds came rushing back to the surface within her. It was not so much her husband's behavior that hurt her so much. It was the fact that she had already been through those things in the past and now the man who said that he loved her and would protect her is demonstrating some of the same hurtful behavior that she had been through before.

We can't put everything on the husband because we have something's within us that need uprooting.

We have to get to the point where we as women have to look at why we expect so much but get so little. One of the reasons we get disappointed and hurt so quickly is because we are looking at the wrong man. He is not Prince charming, he is not perfect, he is not our savior, he is not Mr. Right, he is not a Knight in shining Armor, he is not Denzel Washington or Brad Pitt, and most of all he is not JESUS.

We have to understand who it is that God gave us in marriage. God gave us men of God who are flawed. God has a beautiful sense of humor because He loves using flawed people to bring forth His purpose in life. We are not exempt as women of God to God's way of using flawed people. Yes, that man He gave us is severely flawed!

He is far from perfect. There are many men in ministry that have a super hero complex, especially those who are pastors in the church. We as people make them feel like they are super heroes. People look up to these men of God and cherish the ground that they walk on. Please understand that I am not saying that all of the men of God have this complex but there are a whole lot that do. I know that I am going to get some critical comments on that statement but the truth is the truth.

This super hero complex is why so many of these men behave the way they do in their homes with their wives. They have people coming to them for every little issue in life. They regard themselves as discerning the needs of everyone else but they can't seem to discern the needs of their wives. I heard one preacher say that he was so busy that he preached himself out of his own marriage.

Now don't get it twisted, I understand and agree that men of God deserve to have all the respect that their office calls for. We should honor our husbands and our leaders. I am saying that there are some that let the office of ministry whatever it may be cloud their duties in their own homes.

It reminds me of when my little cousin got his first job as a security guard and they gave him a little flashlight and a uniform. He went around telling people that he was a police. Naw man you are a security guard, now get back to your post.

I knew when I sat down to write this book that it was going to be difficult because I am a pastors wife. I know and understand the struggles of women who are married to pastors who are married to the ministry. Now God did not ordain this. He said that the church is His bride not the bride of the Pastor!

God says that the pastors first ministry is his home.

1 Timothy 3:5 If anyone does not know how to manage his own family, how can he take care of God's church?

One pastor said to me "Pastors rarely feel like they can step away from their ministry responsibilities. They feel "on" 24 hours a day, seven days a week, every day of the year. One pastor explained, "After being an active listener for a lot of other people, I really struggle being interested in my wife and what's going on in her life".

This is part of why there are so many broken ribs in the body of Christ. There is time for everyone else but not enough time for the rib. How can you be so caught up in everyone else's problems and not recognize the needs of those who are in your household? This is another one of those questions that only he will be able to answer. Women we must get to the place where we stop looking at his flaws because his flaws hurt. We are looking at the wrong man, we have to look to Jesus. We have to stop allowing his ways and his flaws to shape how we see ourselves. Your husband may never give you the respect and the love that you need. But you have the power to decide how you define your own life. You can shape it in the image of Christ and all of the wonderful things that He says you are or you can allow your perception of your husband's short comings toward you define who you are.

When I go out from time to time I hear people say "Oh that's the pastors wife" Yes, I am, however that is not my identity. It is important that we as women do not let other people define who we are.

Dr. Tikki A. Collins

I am a woman with many wonderful attributes and contributions. I will not allow anyone to put me in a box to define who I am. Have you seen me? No, you have not seen me. You don't know my struggles, you don't know my battles, you don't know my heart, you only see my scars.

You cannot allow others to put you in a box and decorate you with their ornaments. You are a gift from God and only you and God alone can define you.

As women we sometimes allow our husbands to define who we are. God never intended for our husbands to mold us. God is molding us and he tells us that we are fearfully and wonderfully made.

Psalms 139:14 I will praise thee; for I am fearfully and wonderfully made: marvelous are thy works; and that my soul knoweth right well.

The role of a God fearing husband is to lift up his wife, to love her, to treat her gently and to be effective in pointing her to Christ. It is not to tear her down and mold her into what he wants her to be.

Ephesians 5:25 Husbands, love your wives, even as Christ also loved the church, and gave himself for it;

Let's stop looking at our husbands as the man that we want him to be and start understanding what God wants us to be to the man that He has given us. It's all about us women. After all God said that the man needed help which tells me again that he is incomplete without us. When we are looking at our husbands to be the fixers of our hearts we are looking at the wrong man. He can't fix it no matter how hard he may try.

The fact of the matter is that he will just break it again somewhere down the line. We have to look to Jesus for the healing of our hearts. We are looking at the wrong man when we think that our husband will live up to our expectations however high or low that they may be. Our husbands are not capable of living up to our standards. God tells our husbands to live with us according to his knowledge of God's word to give us honor so that his prayers won't be hindered.

1Pe 3:7 Likewise, ye husbands, dwell with them according to knowledge, giving honor unto the wife, as unto the weaker vessel, and as being heirs together of the grace of life; that your prayers be not hindered.

The reason men of God do not get any further than they are in life or move forward in the desires of their hearts is because they are treating their wives harshly. As I stated earlier, God gives women His word, and he expects us to do what He says for us to do so that we may reap what He is sowing on our behalf. He also gives our husbands the same word and if a husband does not treat his wife right, God says that his prayers will be hindered. Which means that his prayers will be held up if he treats his wife harshly. Now that's deep!

God is looking out for His daughters as He has done all throughout the New Testament. He describes us as the weaker vessel which tells me that He has equipped man to provide for us on all levels. Eve was weak, God tells us that she was deceived not Adam. God says that women need to honored by their husbands as we are the weaker vessel. So what does this mean? When a woman marries a man, she's trusting him with the rest of her life that he won't hit her, cheat on her, that he'll work hard, that he'll pay the bills, that he'll love their family, that he'll finish the race well, that he'll walk with Jesus until the end, that if she gets sick, he'll look after her, that if she is dying, he will be faithful to her. It is a terrifying thing for a woman to trust a sinful man.

I asked a man what he thought about the scripture in 1Peter 3:7 and this is what he said "As a man, I don't think I fully understood this scripture until I had daughters, and now I have some understanding of the fear. The thought of taking one of my daughters and walking them down the aisle and handing them to a man and trusting that he will love them and protect

--

them and serve them and care for them and look after them, it causes me fear and grave concern". WOW, this quote came from a man. He said he never stopped to think about what God was saying in that scripture, what it really meant to honor and protect your wife according to the knowledge of God. This is a part of the problem.

Women have many legitimate fears, we fear being cheated on because it has been done to us by man, we fear being abandoned, we fear being hurt, we have many fears. What Peter is saying is that men need to be a particular way so those fears are alleviated. And I love his words, "in an understanding way, showing honor." That is a man who understands God's heart for a woman. The problem is that every man does not understand his role in a marriage. Women are expected to submit as God tells us to, and ladies we fall short because we don't always do it. The same is true with the husband, he falls short in not understanding his role as a husband as God has laid it out in scripture. Again so many people pat these men on the back because they are super heroes in the public eye at church taking care of everyone else but at home they turn back into Clark Kent and seem to lose their super powers. They don't give their wives the honor that they deserve.

Stop looking at the super hero because you're looking at the wrong man. Start looking at the man who falls short and begin looking at him the way that you envision God wanting him to be according to His word. He may be still living a sinful life but if God said stay.........look at him with the eyes of Hosea, see the man that God is creating through his mess.

See the man that God will call to repentance for every wrong that he has done to you, see the man that God is raising up to be a better man.

If God said to stay in your marriage through your husband's sin, just stand, play your position and watch God bring him to his rightful place as a husband. Keep your eye on the man Jesus and you will be watching the right man.

1 John 4:16 ...God is love. Whoever lives in Love, Lives in God, and God in him.

Chapter 8 Don't Break Up With God

Let's not make the mistake of thinking that somehow God has forgotten about us or have not heard our cry. It's man who makes the mistakes and it is man who causes the disappointment, heartaches and pain.

It is never easy to face marital problems and deal with the pain and wounds that have been inflicted. Hurt, fear and betrayal are real and they hurt us down to the deepest part of our being. If you are committed to staying in your marriage through the good and the bad, you are trusting God to get you to the other side of it, the good.

In order to get back to the good, we must first surrender ourselves to God and the marriage. We must choose to humble ourselves first before God, and then secondly, seek a restorative plan in the marriage that honors God, honors our husband, and puts the relationship above whatever issue we are going through in the marriage. It is so easy to get disconnected and frustrated when you are in a marriage and your husband doesn't seem to care about you or what you are going through. It's hard when he continues to hurt you over and over again.

I want to make it clear that I am not talking about physically being battered. If you are in an abusive relationship being beaten, please leave for your safety. Domestic violence is not to be played with, your life is at stake. I am talking about the hurt that comes with cheating, broken trust, and the many other hurts that plague women in their marriages.

You are not alone. God is your help. Even some of our biblical heroes like David struggled at times to feel God's love in his time of pain. In Psalm 13:1 he cried out,

Psalms 13:1 "How long, O Lord? Will you forget me forever? How long will you hide your face from me?"

When you're feeling as if God doesn't hear you, have you ever cried a prayer like that? I have and I can tell you that it helps me feel connected to God.

I often hear from people who are Christians, but are struggling to feel God's love for them. Their prayers seem to have bounced off the ceiling unanswered. Their cries for God's touch seemed unheard in the heavens. Emptiness had overwhelmed their hearts and left a Godless void inside.

Doubt had driven out faith. If you're going through times like these you may feel like giving up on God, but don't. He hasn't given up on you.

Your problem with God may be a self-esteem problem. Some people feel bad about themselves because of something they did. Others feel bad because of something that was done to them. Either way, don't allow yourself to feel unloved. Work at receiving forgiveness for your short comings and giving forgiveness to those who have hurt you. Don't give in to shame, embarrassment, because of what someone else has done or what has happened to you or your relationship. If you give in to the negative feelings you will feel like hiding just as Eve did in the garden and will tend to shut out God and others who care about you.

Dr. Tikki A. Collins

Instead, dare to believe that you are lovable and worthwhile and that your emotional needs are important. Then look for other women of God to connect with to help get you through some of the difficult times. Fellowship with other women who have overcome the same trials that you are experiencing is a powerful weapon in your arsenal to healing.

If you feel that God is not connecting with you try to examine yourself, see if there is any resentment or bitterness. God says that we must let go of un-forgiveness if we expect to be forgiven. Your problem feeling close to God may be tied to an anger problem. Angry people are lonely people. You may have valid reasons to be angry, but don't stay angry or you'll just hurt yourself. Anger and negativity push people away, even the caring people whom we need.

You can't stay angry at someone and feel their love for you at the same time. If you're angry at God then do what Job did. His children died, his business failed, and he was afflicted with painful boils. Job knew he didn't deserve this pain. Just like you don't deserve the pain that your husband is causing you. Job was angry at God about what had happened to him and all the pain he was in and he told God so. This is the conversation that Job had with God.

"Does it please you [God] to oppress me, to spurn the work of your hands, while you smile on the schemes of the wicked?" Job 10:3

"Surely, O God, you have worn me out; you have devastated my entire household." Job 16:7

"He [God] throws me into the mud, and I am reduced to dust and ashes. I cry out to you, O God, but you do not answer; I stand up, but you merely look at me." Job 30:19-20

"Oh, that I had someone to hear me! I sign now my defense – let the Almighty answer me; let my accuser put his indictment in writing." Job 31:35

"As surely as God lives, who has denied me justice, the Almighty, who has made me taste bitterness of soul…" Job 27:1

Because Job talked through his feelings and let go of his anger he didn't become bitter, he became better. In the end he found God's comfort. You can find God's comfort too if you talk through your anger or resentment with God, let go and trust him, reaching out to him for the love that you need.

Job asked for two things; for his suffering to be taken away, and to be given an audience with God (Job 13:20-22). Then, when he did have an audience with God, he didn't plead his case, and he didn't beg for the suffering to end.

This is why Job is praiseworthy. In the end, the desire to be vindicated was not as strong as his desire to meet with God. Women of God you must have a stronger desire to hear from God for His will for your life then your desire to get your husband right. Once Job had had an encounter with God, his anger disappeared. It was enough to know God and to have been heard by Him. When you meet with God and are confronted by his majesty and goodness, your heart is changed, your knees wobble, your pride falls, the things you were so desperately clinging to fall away.

The questions may still be there but they are asked with a different tone. Learn to talk to God about your healing.

What if Job gave up on God when he didn't hear from God? If Job would have listened to his friends and allowed his situation to dictate Gods plan for his life, he would have never received the wonderful blessing that God had for him in the end. God's word tells us that Job received double for his trouble.

Whatever God is allowing in your marriage, He has equipped you through His mighty word to overcome it and He is looking for you to come to Him the same way Job did. He is looking to heal you and He is looking to give you back everything that you have lost through the process of your pain.

Don't allow your situation to dictate your outcome. Don't keep your eyes fixated on the issues that your husband is bringing your way.

Job didn't focus on his friends he kept talking to God until God showed up. Remember that His timing is not ours. Don't break up with God! Keep talking to God, He hears you, and he cares and He will deliver on His promises to you for your marriage.

Chapter 9 HEALING FROM THE VENOM

A pastors wife fills some pretty big shoes. It's only a special woman that can stand next to a man of God. We ride for our husbands but not every husband will ride for their wife. They may kill for their wife but riding is a different animal.

We as pastors wives have been bitten by the venomous viper of deceit just as Eve was in the Garden of Eden. She was deceived by the serpent, and we are deceived by marriages that has not lived up to the standards of God. Eve was lied to by the serpent saying " Hath not God said" and he followed up with a lie mixed in with the actual word of God.

The same lying serpent has spoken to some of the pastors saying "Hath not God said your wife should be first but only after you finish taking care of everything and everyone else"

Yes, that same devil and his venom is now in the mix of a holy

matrimony. We feel the venom of the bite because we feel the

actions of our husbands. Women of God you go day in and day

out forsaking your needs just to establish his desires for

ministry and you get so little in return. You constantly pour out

but get so little in return. You put up with broken promises,

disappointments, loneliness, and some of you abuse. Through it

all you continue to stagger around feeling at times that no one

understands you, no one knows your pain and no one is there

for you, not even him, the man that said I will cherish you and

love you till death do us part. You ask yourself, what did I get

myself into? How can I be married to a man of God and feel so

lonely.

How can he say he loves God and won't love me the way that God commands him to? How is it that he can so easily pour into everyone else but he comes up empty when I need him emotionally and physically? Why does his passions for everyone else burn so deeply and for me it's just the remnant of the ashes left behind?

We have all been there, we have all asked ourselves some of those questions. We may never get the answers we need from our husbands, but God has the answers we need to heal from the pain.

Don't take his shortcomings on as a burden. The pastor will have to answer to God as to why he did not properly manage the bone of his bone. The pastor or the minister will have to answer to God why his rib was lonely, why she felt neglected because of his lack of attention, why she is hurting and why he did not manage his home well. Just as God asked Adam the question in the garden when Eve tasted the venom and was deceived. God asked Adam "Where are you"

Genesis 3:9 And the LORD God called unto Adam, and said unto him, Where art thou?

God is going to want to know where the pastor is, and why his wife whom God told him to honor as the weaker vessel, why she is feeling abandoned and alone. Why she is being left alone with the venom of despair. Your husband is going to have to answer God just as Adam had to answer God. God sees all that you are going through woman of God, He sees every time your husband puts anything in front of you, he sees every time your husband neglects his duty to you.

He is a God of order and when you maintain your rightful place in Christ, He will go to battle for you. You cannot hide from God. God will get his attention.

Women of God there is healing for you because God has purposed your life for greatness! You will never know what you are made of until God allows you to be tried. This is a trial and God wants to see how well you will overcome the obstacles.

The first thing you have to know is that it is not about your husband, it's all about you! Yes you become one when you are married, but your husband is not going to stand before God for you. You have to make that appearance on your own and when you do God is not going to want to hear that you did not serve him with all that you have because your husband was acting crazy. God is not going for that.

You must allow God to speak to your mind, heart and spirit through these times. The only other option is to have the enemy speak to you and, well we all know how that will end up.

There is a gift so much more precious than diamonds and gold. What's even better is that you can afford to give it to your husband! As a matter of fact if you don't give it, you can't afford to pay the price. This gift will bless you above anything you can ever imagine, it will make you rich beyond measure. It is so rich and precious that you cannot give it in your own strength. Giving it calls for the supernatural power that only Jesus Christ can provide. That gift is forgiveness. Remember it's not for him, it's all for you.

Some women have many hurts left over from previous relationships or lack thereof. We sometimes carry over those hurts and pains into marriage. You don't realize that hurt is still there until your husband does something and you are hurt all over again, and now its worst because this is the man who is suppose to love you. But some of the feelings are escalated by past experiences and it makes the present situation worst.

Sometimes we have not forgiven past hurts and we bring them into our marriages and we don't know how to forgive our husbands. Remember, they think they are super heroes but they are not. Unresolved issues still linger in our hearts at times creating tension and neediness in marriages.

Women of God we often times want a husband that we can look up to spiritually and when he does not show interest in doing that it brings back issues for some of abandonment and feelings of not being loved.

109

We begin to look at his short comings and when he is not living up to your expectation of what you perceive God said he should be doing it causes discord.

We can be very strong and needy at the same time. God really has a great sense of humor. I love for my husband to lead me spiritually but the minute he acts as if he is not interested and drops the ball and I get frustrated waiting on him, I hear my beautiful mother in my ear saying the thing that she has taught me all my life, "If you want something done, do it yourself". Gradually I began making decisions on my own because it appeared that it was what he was comfortable with me doing. The dangerous part comes in when you begin to develop a takeover spirit. This creeps in when your husband leaves you to have to fend for yourself all of the time.

It develops when there is so little attention paid in his home. That's what happened in the garden of Eden. Eve made her own decision.

I understand how this mentality can creep in unaware. This type of independence has been programmed in me as a young girl, so I have brought this mentality with me into my marriage. So many of us get disappointed and disillusioned because our husbands are not the leaders that we have created them to be in our minds. We create a vision and expectation in our mind of what type of leader our husband should be and when he doesn't live up to our perception of what he should be as a leader, we tend to punish him for our disappointments. Your disillusionment with your marriage can cause you to shut yourself off from your husband, both emotionally and physically. This happens because he has not turned out to be the leader you want or imagined him to be so you begin to punish him and yourself for your disappointment by withdrawing into a shell of pride and self-sufficiency. God has no use for pride.

As I sat and listened to the heart of a my good friend Denise as she explained how she became so disenchanted with her husband. She said that she was at her home one day and a woman knocked on her door asking for her husband, Denise said that he was not home at the time and asked the woman who should she say stopped by? The woman asked if Denise was his daughter. Denise was caught off guard even though she was happy to receive such a compliment, but she told the woman that she was his wife. The woman looked very confused and said that she was unaware that he was married.

The woman began to tell Denise that they had been seeing one another for a while and she was just stopping by to say hello. Well of course Denise was angry and began to ask all of the regular questions, you know the questions, how long, where did you meet, are you still seeing him and all the other thousand questions. Denise found out that her husband was no longer seeing this woman, however he had been seeing her throughout their engagement and their courtship. Wow, what a blow!

After Denise's husband returned home, she let him have it. He denied that he had any relationship with this woman and over the next several days he still couldn't muster the courage to say whatever his real involvement was with the woman.

Denise was packing to leave him and he begged her not to go she demanded the truth from him. He began to tell her his hidden sins, and she was shocked and overwhelmed. It seemed unreal—"surely this couldn't be happening to her" she said! Nothing could have prepared her for the waves of bitter reality that she experienced. Her husband had been unfaithful during their engagement, had lied to her, had experienced constant moral failure.

Awakening to Reality.........

Denise was married to a different man than she thought she had been, and her heart became filled with anger and an intense desire for revenge against him. That night, as the storm of despair in her heart raged on, her husband left the house and she was alone with her pain. All of life became a pit of darkness to her, and her joy was taken away.

Denise felt that her husband was worthless, and she didn't see any future in their marriage. Although they had previously committed to never divorce, she felt things were different now and she wanted to be permanently separated from him.

She kept talking it over in her mind as she was now married to a pastor and so many of the people in the church was depending on them. She had to acknowledge that none of her exit plans were pleasing to God and none would benefit the church—She felt trapped with a liar and a deceiver in her marriage. She was bitter and resented her husband.

Denise decided to go face to face again with the woman and get every tawdry detail of the affair. As the woman explained detail by detail every illicit thing that happened in the relationship with her husband she grew even more bitter.

Denise called another pastors wife whom she knew that went through the same thing with her cheating pastor husband. Denise knew that the woman of God would understand because she had been down that road in the past and forgave her husband. Denise began to tell her everything that her husband did and asked her how she could live with such a horrible man. She listened as she poured out her frustration and anger toward her husband. After Denise was finished, the pastors wife said in a gentle and quiet voice, "Well, Denise, what about your own sin?"

Her question shocked Denise—*my* sin? "My husband was the horrible sinner who had hurt me so badly, and I was the innocent victim" she said to the woman. Now she told Denise to look at her own sin? In her mind, her sin didn't even begin to compare with what her husband had done.

She told Denise that she needed to take her eyes off her husband and put them on herself. At first, she was indignant that she would suggest that she look at her own faults. However, she began to help Denise see how she had taken over the role that God had given her husband. She had been disrespectful, self-righteous, and proud. Gradually, God revealed her own sin to her, which was just as bad as her husband's failures. With her eyes taken off her husband's faults, she began to see how great her own sin was, and Denise realized repentance was the only option left to her.

Now God was working in her life—regardless of what her husband was doing. She realized that she had hurt her husband too in many ways, and she began to come to a state of humility and brokenness over her hard heart and disobedience to God as a good wife.

Denise still knew that she had more work to do. She sensed that God wanted something more of her, she knew that she was still holding back some area of her life from God. Still, God continued to prick at her heart. One evening as Denise and her husband sat watching TV, God revealed to her what was missing. She realized that since the affair she had been withholding her heart from her husband. For years she had kept her heart in her own care, sheltering and protecting it from the pain of more disappointment. Now God wanted Denise to give it to her husband freely, with no strings attached. There was no guarantee that her heart would be treated gently, or that her husband would value this gift that was so hard for her to give, but she knew that she wouldn't be free until she surrendered to the Lord.

She gave her husband her heart that night, telling him it was as fragile as glass and asking him to treat it delicately. The joy of release and freedom, which she had not had for many years, now fills her and spills over into every area of life.

Denise allows God to take care of her and she allows God to take care of her husband. As time passes, we all have painful memories that still come to mind. We need to keep reminding ourselves out loud that we too have been forgiven, and we must choose again to forgive and love our husbands regardless of how jacked up they are.

Ephesians 4:31–32 "Let all bitterness, and wrath, and anger, and clamor, and evil speaking, be put away from you, with all malice: And be ye kind one to another, tenderhearted, forgiving one another, even as God for Christ's sake hath forgiven you."

Dr. Tikki A. Collins

True forgiveness is impossible without the supernatural power of Jesus Christ. I remember to ask God daily to make me kind, tender, and forgiving, in all areas of my life. There are amazing change that taken place in my relationships with people. Some people that I could not stand, I can now at least be in the same room with them and treat them kindly. He is creating the deep, heart-to-heart relationship that we are longing for as pastors wives, not only for our marriages but for our greatness as women.

As each day passes, in my own relationship I find God doing a new work in me almost daily. Where coldness and resentment once reigned in my life, I now experience the warmth of Christ's love.

In some areas of my life as a pastors wife, through the situations that used to cause great frustration, I can now work together as a team with my husband.

Sometimes marriages are so mundane and taken for granted that you just exist as roommates forgetting the needs of the other person. My husband and I have certainly not arrived! Both of us are in the process of growing, and we face relational challenges like any other couple. Currently, the Lord is teaching me how to love my husband the way he needs to be loved.

We are still learning and growing after 5 years of marriage! We trust His grace to keep us free and to continue to purify us. The best thing about my marriage is that we both love Jesus and we love one another. I have learned that perfect love cast out all fear. Don't be afraid to give your heart to your husband, God picks up any broken pieces.

There is hope for your marriage! God can take an impossible and miserable situation and turn it into a beautiful relationship that is filled with joy. It begins with you, your healing, your willingness to be restored.

You must believe that God can and trust that God will.

the JOY of the LORD is your strength.

Nehemiah 8:10

Chapter 9 GET YOUR LIFE

It's time to get your life! It's time for you to look within and grab

on to the things that God has called you to do. As I talked to one

of the pastors wives who I will call Kelly she shared with me the

hardship of being lonely when her husband was called away to

his many, many meetings. She said " this evening is my

husband's monthly elders meeting again! So ONCE again I'll be

left behind, and once again try to be creative in how to keep

myself occupied. But how well will I manage my attitude THIS

time? Will I let the Lord wash me with patience and

contentment for a husband I love dearly doing a work I believe

in? Or will the loneliness of an evening in the house spark

resentment, and sadness? Or will I reach for my Bible and let

the Lord keep me company? Or will I allow my discontentment

to make bad choices"?

Each one of us as pastors wives have a feeling of being left out or alone more than we should be. There is more times than not that he puts all things ministry before you and you wait angrily for the little morsel of time that he may carve out of his day for you. You continue to wait, and wait, and wait. Loneliness starts to settle in.

Jesus, too, felt loneliness at times, more so when he was being persecuted and placed on a cross. A most painful time in his life. His most faithful followers abandoned him in his hour of need. The people who followed him and loved him before he was crucified were no longer there for him.

He knew exactly what it felt like to be alone, and so He knows exactly what we go through when we feel loneliness.

But what are you doing with the time while you wait? God has given you that time. What desires and gifts has God placed within you? What are your goals in life? What ministry did he set in your heart? It's time to fill your emptiness with the gifts of God.

Only you and God know what you are passionate about. You must replace that lonely space with the gifts and desires that God has placed within you. This is your time to "Get your life"! This is a time for you to discover that you have a voice outside of that of your husband's shadow. If you don't know what your gifts are, pray and ask God to reveal your purpose.

It's not like God is trying to hide His will from us or that He will not help us find His will for our lives.

Just read Ephesians 1:11, *"In him we were also chosen, having been predestined according to the plan of him who works out everything in conformity with the purpose of his will."*

Everything will work out for our good and things in our life will be according to "the purpose of his will.

 Romans 8:28 confirms "that in all things God works for the good of those who love him, who have been called according to his purpose." God never asked us to sit around and wither up.

I have decided to use my time to be a voice to other pastors wives. God has given me something to say through my experiences. If you never have those difficult times of being and feeling alone, you may never have the time to think on the goodness of God and the things that he wants you to do.

We often use the time that our husbands are away to feel alone and resentment. That combination is only disaster waiting to happen. Again I say, your husband will have to answer to God for not putting you first. The ministry is not his wife, however it's going to take God to show him that.

Meanwhile you have to get your life. Find what you love to do and get to doing it. Make plans to become the best you that God has for you to become. There is greatness in every woman, she just has to discover it. We are so awesome that God says it's not good for man to be without us! Put your mark on the world.

Challenge yourself spiritually. Find someone who spiritually challenges you, who encourages you to love God more. She inspires you to be the best woman you can be.

She helps you stay disciplined and helps you try to improve in areas of your life. Look for a mentor that is a little bit further along in her walk with God, a role model of a Christian wife. Everyone needs a friend who makes her feel happy and uplifted each time you're together. She gives you perspective, because she takes your mind off of your challenges. You laugh when you're together. This woman sees the rainbow behind the cloud. Though she may never know the details of your life or ministry, her role is to remind you that *joy* is available for you and you can achieve the greatness that God has set before you.

Woman of God you can rest in the fact that God is sovereign over everything that happens in this life. He directs events, He puts people in our paths, and essentially He enables us to be in the right place at the right time.

Proverbs 21:1 is one of my favorite Scriptures for reassurance when I am praying for God's will in my life, *"The king's heart is like channels of water in the hand of the LORD; He turns it wherever He wishes."* If God can direct the king's heart to "wherever He wishes", then surely He can direct you to the where He wants you to go or whatever His will is for you. The key here is that *your* will must be aligned with *His* will or you will be frustrated.

We already know that God's will is for us to not be conformed to this world, to be renewed in our minds by the Holy Spirit, and to seek godly counselors, but He also wants us to know that He is directing your life in His good and pleasing sovereignty for what is best for you. He wants you to trust Him in this directing or redirecting.

There is a ministry waiting to be birthed in you through these trials. Use this time to go higher in the things of God. There is something in you waiting to birthed to become a blessing to you and someone else.

Ephesians 2:10 For we are his workmanship, created in Christ Jesus for good works, which God prepared beforehand, that we should walk in them.

You are a wonderful woman and God gave you purpose!

I *Know* My PURPOSE

Chapter 11   A LETTER TO THE PASTOR FROM HIS WIFE

This letter is to our husbands from your leading ladies.

Hi honey we know it's hard carrying all of those burdens

around. We understand that you are God's shepherd and your

trying your best to live up to your calling. We know that

ministry is hard and it requires wisdom, sacrifice, time and

energy. We want you to know that it's also hard on us. Yes, we

know that the burden you carry is huge but please don't forget

that we have to watch you carry it which creates a huge burden

for us to carry. You are discouraged many days and nights and

no one even knows but you and God. We watch as you

intercede for people and carry their problems, we see how you

are talked about and criticized at times, yet we have to endure

the pain that comes along with watching you be talked about

and hurt while trying to figure out how to encourage you and at the same time still loving the person without punching them in the face. You bear the burden of balancing your family at home with the burdens of the ministry and we are left to use wisdom figuring out how to let you do the things of the ministry and how much to encourage you to draw boundaries to protect your relationship with your wife and family.

We have the unique challenge of trying to be gracious with your crazy schedules. We struggle not only with our own battles, but also with the awareness of your burden for the flock. We know how much it hurts when someone strays, the energy that you put out with a family in crisis, the hours you spend in preparing to feed the sheep.

We have come to realize that probably our biggest challenge of all has just been to let our husband know when we are feeling overwhelmed with our life and have him actually listen.

The last thing we want to do is add one more burden to your plate because we know that you are carrying so much.

Yet there are times when life is just hard for us too, and we are in this together after all. We need your love, support and your time as much as anyone else, even more. We are the ones that care when everyone else walks out. We are the ones that are constant. Members can be like a revolving door and we watch as the same scenario plays out year after year with people coming and people going. We are at your side year after year member after member. We watch as you labor so intensely with other peoples burdens even praying you through it. We watch as the congregation make plans with their families and spouses to do fun things all while imagining in our minds what it would be like to spend time like that with you. We get what's left of you most of the time, which isn't all ways much but we try to be happy with that. We would be happy playing second to God, we just get tired playing second to everyone else all the time. See we know that God says to take care of your home first and then the church. We are praying and wanting the time, attention and energy that you give to others to be given to us.

So Pastor, honey we want you to know that we will continue to pray for your needs and pray to God that we will be sensitive to your needs, that we will be wise in our counsel, that we will be gentle with our tongue and that our home will always be one where you are happy to return to.

Pastor we also ask that you will pray for us not just as a member of the flock but also as flesh of your flesh bone of your bone remembering that we are one and we are carrying these burdens together. Without your love and support the rib is easily broken.

Please God remind him that we are precious in your site.

From a Pastors mouth...........

"Men — we must love and lead our wives before we love and lead the church. You will always disappoint someone; so choose to disappoint others and not the wife of your youth. The others will come and go. They will soon forget the disappointment you caused. They will likely one day forget about you, too. Your marriage is very different — it is "till death do us part."

"Quote Anonymous "

Chapter 12   Joy Comes In The Morning

To come to God the Father you must have humility and respect.

Yelling at God our Father, making demands that He has to do

what you want is not the way.

Do not throw in the towel with your spouse. I had the biggest

inner battle that I thought I had gotten rid of. But guess what; it

hit me again this summer. I learned that when we come before

God our Father with a sincere heart with total respect, He will

lead us through the pages of our Bible and start to show us

where we need to improve. It is not going to be easy at all.

When praying, not only do we ask for humility, we ask for

courage, strength, faith, and His righteous love. His love is

forgiveness. He can see into everyone's hearts and He knows

where you hurt.

Hold on to the hope and promise that He can and will redeem this disaster. And in the mean time we have to learn what it is to suffer rejection, betrayal, injustice....just as our Savior did.

I get it now... how incredible it is that Jesus forgave and loved the people who hurt him. Some of our hearts are still broken but we must keep praying for a rescue. It draws us closer and rebuilds a new friendship with Jesus.

"Let your requests be made known to God, with thanksgiving, and the peace of God, which surpasses all understanding will guard your hearts and minds through Christ Jesus" (Philippians 4:6-7).

"Finally, brethren, whatever things are true, whatever things are noble, whatever things are just, whatever things are pure, whatever things are lovely, whatever things are of good report, if there is any

virtue and if there is anything praiseworthy—meditate on these things" (Philippians 4:8).

"Blessed be the God and Father of our Lord Jesus Christ, the Father of mercies and God of all comfort, who comforts us in all our tribulation, that we may be able to comfort those who are in any trouble, with the comfort with which we ourselves are comforted by God. For as the sufferings of Christ abound in us, so our consolation also abounds through Christ. Now if we are afflicted, it is for your consolation and salvation, which is effective for enduring the same sufferings which we also suffer. Or if we are comforted, it is for your consolation and salvation. And our hope for you is steadfast, because we know that as you are partakers of the sufferings, so also you will partake of the consolation" (2 Corinthians 1:3-7).

Suffering is a way to help us grow stronger, to bring us closer to God and mature in dealing with life's situation.

I know it is easier said than done for us who are weathering the storms right now. But God's grace will heal our wounds. Never forget, whatever pain and suffering we have right now, our Lord Jesus has experienced it and He knows what we are going through.

Your joy is in Christ Jesus. Joy is not something, it is SOMEONE. *Jesus said in John 15:11"These things have I spoken unto you, that my JOY might be in you and that your joy might be full."*

Joy is not determined by circumstances. Jesus the night before He was crucified looked at His disciples and said, "My joy I give unto you, not as the world gives but such as I have given unto thee." In a few hours He was going to be hanging from a blood soaked cross. He would be plunged into a sea of suffering like no other man had experienced before, yet He turns His face from the upper room and looks into the shadows of Gethsemane and He looks into the darkness of unspeakable agony and He says to His disciples, "My joy I give unto you..." Jesus gave you your joy and no man can take it from you. The only way someone can take your joy is if you hand it to him on a silver platter and say, "here, you control me, you take my joy, I give it to you."

Weeping may endure for a night but joy will come in the morning. Joy comes with knowing that God will show up in the morning with a fresh new opportunity for you to let go and start all over. Fear may linger for the night, anger may linger for a night, grief may linger for a night, pain may linger for a night, but, "Joy cometh in the morning"!

My Prayer for pastors wives.........

Father, I lift up my co-laborers, your daughters to You asking You to give them an extra measure of joy today. Joy that comes from recognizing You in their situation. Increase their faith today by experiencing Your presence in their comings and goings.

There is nothing I want more for them than to know You as the God of the here and now and not the God of the far away. Be real to them, Father, in a way they have never experienced and may their eyes be open to your fingerprints around them. Continue to hold them through the absence of their husbands and the trials that come their way. Remind them that you will

never let them fall. Bless their husbands and anoint them with

an abundance of love for their wives. Allow their hearts to act

upon the love that you ordained for marriage in your word.

Speak to our hearts Lord, don't allow bitterness and the serpent

of the garden to deceive our minds. Our healing is in your

hands and in your hands we have joy. Your daughters love you

Jesus! Amen

Dr. Tikki Collins is a Christian radio host and can be heard anywhere in the world live on the air on iHeart Radio!

Listen today to "Lord Put A Ring On It"

Download the iHeart app in the Google Play Store or itunes.

iHeartRadio

Just For you Ladies! Download your free, Lord Put A Ring On It App from the Google Play store.

Contact info: www.Lordputaringonit.com

email: Lordputaringonit@mail.com

www.ingramcontent.com/pod-product-compliance
Lightning Source LLC
Chambersburg PA
CBHW072022040426
42447CB00009B/1695